The
Reverse
Mortgage
Handbook

A Consumer's Guide
for
Senior Homeowners

T.E. Ballman

First Edition
Jawbone Publishing - Kissimmee, Florida

The Reverse Mortgage Handbook

Published by:
Jawbone Publishing Corporation
Kissimmee, FL
http://www.JawbonePublishing.com

Author Contact Information:
Tara Ballman
P.O. Box 137621
Clermont, FL 34713
Email: Tara@ReverseMortgageHandbook.com

ISBN: 1-59094-055-5
Copyright © 2004, by Tara Ballman
Printed in the United States of America

Library of Congress Cataloging-in-Publication Data
Ballman, T. E. (Tara E.), 1976-
 The reverse mortgage handbook: a consumer's guide for senior homeowners / T.E. Ballman.-- 1st ed.
  p. cm.
 ISBN 1-59094-055-5 (pbk.) -- ISBN 1-59094-056-3 (large print pbk.)
 1. Mortgage loans, Reverse--United States--Handbooks, manuals, etc. 2. Home equity conversion--United States--Handbooks, manuals, etc. 3. Aged--Housing--United States--Finance--Handbooks, manuals, etc. I. Title.
HG2040.5.U5B353 2003
332.7'22--dc22

The Reverse Mortgage Handbook
Table of Contents

Acknowledgements

I offer a most sincere thank you to the following people for their assistance and encouragement:

Tom Scabareti, VP - Marketing & Communications,
    Financial Freedom Senior Funding,Inc;
Jeffrey S. Taylor, CMB, VP - Senior Products Group,
    Wells Fargo Home Mortgage, Inc.;
David Carey, Product Manager,
    Fannie Mae;
Sandra Cutts, Senior Media Relations Manager,
    Fannie Mae;
Glenn Petherick, Director of Communications,
    National Reverse Mortgage Lenders Association (NRMLA);
Tom Bales, President,
    Seminole Funding, Inc.; and

A special thanks to my parents - **Swanee Ballman**, who always encouraged me to write from a young age, and **Frank Ballman**, who had a great idea about a book!

Note to Reader

Although reverse mortgages have been available since the early 1960's, the program didn't gain popularity until 1987, when the federally-insured Home Equity Conversion Mortgage (HECM) developed by the Department of Housing and Urban Development brought stability to the program. Two years later, Fannie Mae began purchasing reverse mortgages and eventually released the Home Keeper reverse mortgage in 1996.

Numerous reverse mortgage products have been on the market since its inception. Today, there are only three major products available:

- HUD's federally-insured Home Equity Conversion Mortgage,
- Fannie Mae's proprietary Home Keeper Mortgage, and
- Financial Freedom's proprietary Cash Account™.

Disclaimer

This handbook is designed to provide information on reverse mortgages. It is sold with the understanding that the publisher and author are not engaged in rendering legal, financial or other professional services. If legal or other expert assistance is required, the services of a competent professional should be sought.

It is not the purpose of this manual to reprint all the information that is otherwise available, but to complement, amplify and supplement other texts. You are urged to read all available material, learn as much information as possible about reverse mortgages, and tailor the information to your individual needs.

Every effort has been made to make this manual as complete and as accurate as possible. However, there may be mistakes in content. Therefore, this text should be used only as a general guide and not as the ultimate source of reverse mortgage information. This handbook contains information on reverse mortgages that is current only up to the publication date. The author and publisher assume no responsibility for errors, inaccuracies, omissions, or inconsistencies.

The purpose of this handbook is to educate. The author and publisher shall have neither liability nor responsibility to any person or entity with respect to any loss or damage caused, or alleged to have been caused, directly or indirectly, by the information contained in this book. The author and publisher are not endorsing any reverse mortgage product, option or lender.

If you do not wish to be bound by the above, you may return this book to the publisher for a refund.

Contact Information

If you would like to contact the author to ask a reverse mortgage related questions, request additional information, or schedule a speaking engagement, please send all correspondence to:

The Reverse Mortgage Handbook
Tara Ballman
P.O. Box 137621
Clermont, FL 34713

Email: Tara@ReverseMortgageHandbook.com
Website: www.ReverseMortgageHandbook.com

If you would like to contact the publisher for any reason, please send all correspondence to:

Jawbone Publishing Corporation
2907 Paddington Way
Kissimmee, FL 34747

Telephone: (407) 396-4245
Fax: (407) 396-4247

Website: www.JawbonePublishing.com
Email: Marketing@JawbonePublishing.com

Heading Forward in Reverse

Most homeowners understand traditional or "forward" mortgage basics. A mortgage company loans you money to purchase your home. As you pay your monthly interest and principal payments, the equity in your home increases and your debt decreases. Simple.

Once a monthly mortgage payment is made, homeowners are offered only a few options to draw from their home's equity:

- Sell the home,
- Refinance the mortgage, or
- Apply for a home equity loan.

Selling the home may not always be the preferred option. Refinancing and home equity loans require monthly repayments plus income verification to ensure that the loan will be repaid.

For those age 62 or over, another special option is available. Homeowners remain in their homes, retain the property's title, and receive tax-free funds without making monthly repayments. This is called a reverse mortgage. It may also be considered a zero-payment home loan, since no monthly mortgage repayments are required.

With a forward mortgage, you and your home begin with a large amount of debt and very little equity. Through the years as you make monthly payments, your debt decreases as your equity (cash invested in your home) increases. As you pay your mortgage, the cash invested in your house transforms into equity.

As the name implies, a reverse mortgage is just the opposite of a forward mortgage. Homeowners convert a portion of the equity in their homes into cash. Since you retain the title to your home throughout the life of the reverse mortgage, **you** own your home - not the bank or mortgage lender. And, you will <u>never</u> owe more than the value of your home because the amount due can never exceed the home's value. No exceptions!

How homeowners spend the cash does not require any explanation. It may be used to supplement monthly income, develop a line of credit, cover medical expenses, or to simply enjoy an increased quality of life throughout the retirement years.

Quick Facts

1. Reverse mortgages access the equity in your home.

2. No monthly payments are required with reverse mortgages.

3. You retain the title to your home.

4. You may never owe more than the value of your home.

Reverse mortgages include numerous safety measures to protect seniors and their homes. After the final paperwork is signed at closing (and the reverse mortgage closing involves just as much paperwork as a traditional "forward" mortgage), the applicants still have three days to change their minds without legal obligation. (This is called a three-day right of rescission.)

Since many homeowners have spent a lifetime paying off a mortgage and building a place to call "home", the possibility of losing their home is a major concern. However, since you don't have to make monthly repayments on the reverse mortgage, you don't have to worry about missing a payment and losing your home. Again, you retain the title to your home. The bank or lender will not own it!

In the past, some senior citizens have been charged thousands of dollars for reverse mortgage information that is available free. Some companies call it "estate planning" fees. Beware of any company that charges a fee for simply receiving information! HUD has directed all HECM lenders to stop doing business with companies that charge such fees.

More of the federally-mandated safeguards are reviewed in detail in Chapter 7.

Tax-Free Funds

The income you receive through a reverse mortgage is not taxed; the money is already yours. These are the funds you have paid on your mortgage throughout the years. Therefore, you are not actually earning income from the reverse mortgage.

Because you are not earning income, benefits from non-need based programs such as regular Social Security and Medicare benefits should not be affected. If you receive Supplemental Social Security (SSI), Medicaid, AFDC, food stamps, or any other need-based income, reverse mortgage funds may affect your benefits (if the money is not spent in the same month it is received). Be sure to contact a benefits specialist, your local Area Agency on Aging, or a financial counselor for confirmation of your benefits' safety.

If you are purchasing an annuity with your reverse mortgage funds, annuity advances are considered income under Supplemental Security

Income (SSI) and Medicaid programs. Thus, an annuity may also affect your benefits.

Use of Reverse Mortgage Funds

You may use your reverse mortgage funds in any manner you wish. Common uses are:

- To pay rising health care costs,
- Supplement monthly retirement income,
- Purchase long term care insurance,
- Make home improvements or modifications,
- Pay off an existing mortgage or other debt,
- Purchase a new car,
- Travel,
- Gift to children or grandchildren, or
- Funding college tuition.

Eligibility Requirements

All reverse mortgage products have the same general eligibility requirements.

Age Requirement

You must be at least 62 years old. In the case of co-borrowers, if both names appear on the home's title (which is usually a spouse), both must be 62. If a co-borrower is under 62, the younger borrower must be removed from the title for the property to be eligible. (This may involve serious ramifications for the younger borrower and should first be discussed with a counselor and/or your attorney! This is discussed in more detail in Chapter 6 – Special Circumstances.)

Residence Requirement

The property must be your primary residence, and you must live in the house over 6 months out of a year. You may not claim the property as your primary residence if you have not occupied the property for a period of 12 consecutive months because of a physical or mental illness.

Eligible properties include:
- Single family homes,
- Condominiums,
- Manufactured homes,
  (except Financial Freedom's Cash Account™)
- Modular homes, and
- One-to-four unit rentals (if owner occupies one unit).

Ineligible properties include:
- Co-ops
  (except in New York City),
- Second homes,
- Commercial properties, and
- Agricultural properties.

Consumer Education Requirement

All reverse mortgage products require applicants to receive one-time consumer education, at no cost to you, before the loan process may begin. You may meet with a lender to discuss costs and benefits and sign the initial disclosure forms, but the lender may not charge you for any service or fee until you have completed the counseling, obtained a counseling certificate (valid for 180-days), and the lender has your original certificate on file.

Equity Requirement

You must be a homeowner with equity in your primary residence. Even if you have an outstanding mortgage balance, you may still qualify for a reverse mortgage. However, all debts or liens on your residence must be paid *before* you may receive any reverse mortgage funds. (In many cases, these debts will be paid at closing with your funds before you receive them.)

Reverse mortgages must be "first" mortgages, meaning there cannot be any other debt against the home. If you have a current mortgage balance or a home equity loan, your reverse mortgage funds will pay these loans first. You will receive any remaining funds.

In some cases, this is the goal of the homeowner – to eliminate monthly mortgage payments. However, if your mortgage balance is high compared to the value of your home (loan to value percentage), you will not be eligible to participate in the reverse mortgage program.

Since you will not be making monthly payments, your income level and credit score will not affect the amount of money you receive. So, if you are retired and living on a limited income, that information has absolutely no effect on the decision to award you a reverse mortgage.

However, lenders will check your credit to research the following information: bankruptcies, tax liens, outstanding student loans, oustanding mortgage balance, and any judgments.

Bankruptcies

All bankruptcies must be dismissed or discharged. The only

exception is a Chapter 13 bankruptcy that you may pay off at closing. Or, you may obtain written permission from the court and signed by a judge that states you may continue with the reverse mortgage although the Chapter 13 is still active. (If you are paying off a Chapter 13 bankruptcy, or if you have a dismissed or discharged Chapter 13 within the last two years, you may be required to sign a bankruptcy certificate.)

Tax Liens

All tax liens must be paid at your reverse mortgage closing.

Student Loans

Any delinquent students loans must be paid at closing.

Outstanding Mortgage

If you currently have a mortgage balance, it must be paid at closing before you receive any funds.

Judgments

If the judgment is a lien against the property, it must be paid at closing. If the judgment is not against the property, it will not affect your reverse mortgage, unless it is a federal debt.

Home Condition Requirements

As part of the reverse mortgage process, an appraisal of your home will be completed. Your lender will send an approved appraiser, who must inspect your home's interior and exterior. If the appraiser notes any deterioration, you may be required to correct the problem before you receive your reverse mortgage funds or establish a repair escrow.

Potential repairs could range from termite damage to painting the exterior of the house. (See the "Required Repairs" section in Chapter 6).

Insurance Requirements

Both HUD and Fannie Mae require hazard (or homeowners) insurance, which must be equal to the appraised value of the home.

If you currently have hazard insurance, but it is not equal to the appraised value of your home, you may obtain "Guaranteed Replacement Coverage". This replacement coverage will guarantee the difference between your appraised value and your insured amount.

Depending on your location, flood insurance may be required for the life of the loan. Flood insurance is based on the appraised value minus the site value, or there may be a maximum flood insurance limit for your area. The Federal Emergency Management Agency (FEMA) determines if you are required to have flood insurance.

In most cases, you may pay the flood insurance premium at closing with your reverse mortgage proceeds. This way, if you decide you do not want a reverse mortgage, you will not have purchased insurance that you do not need.

Title insurance is required and based on the principal loan amount. This insurance financially protects the lender against a legally defective title, ensuring the lender the title is marketable and free and clear of any problems.

Borrower's Medical History

Reverse mortgages do not require a medical examine, nor is your medical history of any importance.

Available Funds

The amount available to every homeowner depends upon:

- Applicant's age,
- Home value,
- Geographic location,
- Current interest rates, and
- Type of reverse mortgage product.

The maximum reverse mortgage amount, also called the principal limit, is the total amount of funds an applicant is eligible to receive. Typically, the principal limits falls between 25 to 65 percent of your home's value.

For calculation purposes, reverse mortgage products assume a 100-year life expectancy. Therefore, the older the borrower, the more money for which they qualify. Also, the higher the home is valued, the more money for which the borrower might qualify.

When you speak with a reverse mortgage lender, ask to review a comparison sheet of all available reverse mortgage plans. Your lender is required by law to provide this to you. In some cases, the amount for which you qualify through various plans could differ by tens of thousands of dollars.

For specific figures for your situation, you will need to speak with a qualified reverse mortgage lender. If you have internet access, a free reverse mortgage calculators is available on the following websites to calculate an estimated figure:

AARP - www.aarp.org/revmort

National Reverse Mortgage Lenders Association
www.nrmla.org

Disbursement Options

Reverse mortgage funds are available in several options. You may receive:

- An immediate lump sum in cash,
- A pre-determined monthly cash payment as long as your reside in the home as your primary residence (or tenure plan),
- A term plan,
- A line of credit, or
- A combination of the above.

Before making your disbursement decision, be sure to weigh the pros-and-cons of each option. Every situation is different. You may change your plan at any time, but a nominal fee may be charged. (At the time of publication, residents of Texas were not able to use the line of credit option, per state law.)

If you select an immediate lump sum, you may receive all of your available reverse mortgage funds in one payment, usually disbursed on the first day of your loan (which begins after the three-day right of rescission). If you take all of your available funds in a one-time lump sum payment, you will not receive any additional funds under the reverse mortgage program, even if the value of your home increases (unless you decide to refinance your reverse mortgage).

If you opt for a tenure plan, you will receive a pre-determined amount of funds every month until you no longer occupy the home as your primary residence. If you plan on living in your home for the remainder of your life, you will receive the monthly payments as long as you live. You may receive your monthly payment as a check or deposited directly into your checking account.

REAL LIFE EXAMPLE 1-1

Homeowner's Age: 70
Home Value: $150,000
Mortgage Balance: -0-
Expected Interest Rate: 5.77%

FHA/HUD Monthly Adjustable
Net Available: $ 87,897.92
Potential Monthly Payments: $ 539.53
Creditline Growth Rate: 3.29%

FHA/HUD Annually Adjustable
Net Available: $ 79,854.81
Potential Monthly Payments: $ 521.34
Creditline Growth Rate: 3.89%

Fannie Mae's Home Keeper
Net Available: $ 44,164.12
Potential Monthly Payments: $ 319.31
Creditline Growth Rate: -0-

Standard Cash Account
Net Available: $ 32,425.07
Potential Monthly Payments: $ -0-
Creditline Growth Rate: 5%

Zero Point Cash Account
Net Available: $ 35,524.07
Potential Monthly Payments: $ -0-
Creditline Growth Rate: 5%

Based on rates from Janary 17, 2004. Changes in applicant's age, home value, geographic location, and interest rate may cause available amounts to increase or decrease.

A term plan provides equal monthly payments every month for a specific number of months. For example, you may want to receive all of your reverse mortgage funds over the course of 7 months or 7 years. You decide the length of the term.

A line of credit, which is similar to a savings account, allows you to use your reverse mortgage funds whenever you desire - without scheduled payments or installations - until the line of credit is exhausted. The amount of cash you withdraw from your line of credit is the amount of debt determined in your loan (plus fees and interest).

With some reverse mortgage products, the unused funds in your line of credit will have a monthly or annual growth rate. The unused funds is not actually making money; the growth rate allows you access to more of your home's equity.

If the outstanding balance on your line of credit reaches the credit limit, your lender may refuse to make additional extensions of credit. This is similar to reaching your credit limit with a credit card.

You may also combine disbursement plans to suit your particular needs. For example, you might need an immediate lump sum payment that does not use the total amount of funds available to you. You may combine the two options by taking the lump sum payment and placing the remaining funds in a line of credit.

There are exceptions to the above disbursement options with Financial Freedom's Cash Account product (see Chapter 5).

Using Real Life Example 1-1, let's assume the homeowner decides the FHA/HUD Monthly Adjustable is the best option for his situation. Real Life Example 1-2 reviews some of the choices available with this plan.

REAL LIFE EXAMPLE 1-2

FHA/HUD Monthly Adjustable

Net Available: $ 87,897.92
Potential Monthly Payments: $ 539.53
Creditline Growth Rate: 3.29%

Examples of Disbursement Options

$ 87,897.92 as cash lump sum

- or -

$ 539.53 a month as long as homeowner
maintains primary residence

- or -

$3,886.09 a month for 24 months
(term payment)

- or -

$ 20,000 as cash lump sum and
$ 67,897.92 in a line of credit
(with 3.29% growth)

- or-

$15,000 as cash lump sum
$ 15,000 as line of credit
$ 355.38 a month as long as homeowner
maintains primary residence

Based on 5.77% expected interest rate. Changes in applicant's age, home value, geographic location, and interest rates may cause available amounts to increase or decrease.

Determining Interest Rates

Each reverse mortgage product has its own way of determining interest rates. You will find more information about calculating interest in each product's chapter (Chapter 2 for HECM, Chapter 3 for Fannie Mae, and Chapter 4 for Financial Freedom's Cash Account).

Reverse mortgages have accrued interest, meaning the interest charges accumulate over a period of time. You are not obligated to pay the interest until your loan period is over.

Termination

The reverse mortgage becomes due and payable when you no longer occupy the home as your primary residence. This could be due to death, illness, or a move to a new home. If you have a joint reverse mortgage (i.e., husband and wife), the loan is not due until the last surviving borrower permanently leaves the residence.

Under the reverse mortgage program, your lender may require payment of the outstanding reverse mortgage balance if one of the following takes place:
- The last surviving borrower has passed away;
- All borrowers sold or transferred the title to the property;
- The property is no longer the primary residence of at least one borrower;
- One of the borrowers has not occupied the property for a period of over 1 year due to physical or mental illness;
- The property requires repairs, and the borrower does not comply; and/or
- Taxes and insurance have not been paid.

(Several of the above items are also general requirements, or "conditions of default" with traditional mortgages.)

In the event of an illness that requires the last surviving homeowner to permanently change residential locations, the home is no longer considered the primary residence. If this scenario occurs, the reverse mortgage will be due.

If you allow your property to deteriorate beyond normal and reasonable wear and tear, you will be required to correct the problem. These repairs can range from such issues as a leaky roof to termite damage. If you do not correct the problem in a timely manner, your reverse mortgage loan will be due. Since you can never owe more than the value of your home, this deterioration will decrease the value of your property and could cause the lender to lose money.

As with a traditional mortgage, you are required to pay your property taxes, hazard insurance, and, if necessary, flood insurance. You do have the option of allowing the lender to pay these fees (out of your reverse mortgage funds), or you may pay them yourself. If you opt for the lender to pay these items, it will reduce the amount of funds available to you because lenders set-aside the funds in advance. However, if you fail to pay these fees, you will be in violation of your reverse mortgage agreement and the loan will be due.

Your lender may also refuse to provide additional extensions of credit if:

- The outstanding balance on your line of credit reaches the credit limit (principal limit);
- The lender has notified you of termination for one of the six reasons previously listed;
- A petition for bankruptcy has been filed by or against you; or
- You have paid your outstanding balance in full.

Certain issues may also affect the security of your loan. Your reverse mortgage may become due and payable if you:

- Rent a part of your home,
- Add a new owner to the title,
- Change your home's zoning classification, or
- Acquire new debt against your home.

Repayment

You, or your estate, will have 30 days to notify your lender of the sale of your house, a transfer of primary residence, or the death of the last surviving borrower. You must then inform your lender of the means you will use to repay the reverse mortgage. Up to six months is available for you to sell or refinance the home. After six months, if you have approval from the lender, you may obtain extensions in 90 days increments. However, the limit for repayment is 1 year.

Reverse mortgages are non-recourse loans. This means that the lender cannot require repayment based on anything other than your home's value. Therefore, the total amount due is limited to the total value of your home. So, you do not need to be concerned with passing along any excess reverse mortgage debt to your heirs or estate.

By the end of the agreement, you will owe the lender the total amount funded, accrued interest, accrued mortgage insurance premiums (for HECM only), servicing fees (reviewed in Chapter 8 - Costs), and any fees that were financed into your reverse mortgage.

If your home is passed to heirs, the requirements for the reverse mortgage balance must be paid in a similar manner to the requirements for a traditional mortgage: either through personal funds, a traditional mortgage, or the sale of the home. If the house is sold, your heirs will keep any excess funds once the revere mortgage has been satisfied. The home does not have to be sold, but the loan must be repaid in one lump sum.

Regardless of the reason, when the time comes to repay the reverse mortgage, it must be repaid in one payment – either from the sale of your home or other means.

CHAPTER 1 SUMMARY

Eligibility Requirements
- Minimum Age – 62 years
- Must own property
- Property must be primary residence
- Participate in counseling

Reverse Mortgage Loan Limit
- HECM varies by location between $161,076 - $290,319
- Fannie Mae's limit $333,700
- Financial Freedom's Cash Account™ has no limit

Disbursement Options
- Cash lump sum
- Tenure payment
- Term payment
- Line of credit
- Combination of the above

Borrower's Responsibilities
- Pay taxes & insurance
- Maintain property
- Occupy home as primary residence

Repayment
- Up to 6 months is available to sell or refinance the home
- With lenders approval, extensions in 90 day increments
- Must be repaid in one payment within a maximum one year period

2 Home Equity Conversion Mortgage

All reverse mortgage products have the same basic function – to allow you to tap into your home's equity and receive funds in a predetermined manner. Depending on your circumstances, you may receive a certain amount of money from one option and a smaller amount from another.

The option you chose is significant. Without knowledge of all available options, you could receive thousands of dollars less.

HECM Product Profile

The Home Equity Conversion Mortgage, or HECM, is the only reverse mortgage program insured by the federal government. It is available through the Federal Housing Administration (FHA), a division of the U.S. Department of Housing & Urban Development (HUD).

Over 95 percent of all reverse mortgage borrowers choose the HECM product. What makes this option so popular? FHA provides insurance. (And, unless you have a high valued home, you generally get more money.) Because the Federal government insures this product, it is considered the safest reverse mortgage product currently available.

Mortgage insurance is a safety measure that ensures you will always receive your reverse mortgage funds as long as you maintain primary residence in that particular home. For example, if your lender refuses to continue monthly payments, or if your lender is no longer in business, you would continue to receive your monthly payments through FHA.

Mortgage insurance also protects the lender; it ensures that the lending institution will receive the total repayment of the reverse mortgage balance, even if your home's value is less than the total amount due. As long as you occupy the home as your primary residence, you will not be forced to sell. The FHA insurance guarantees that the lender will receive its full payment, and neither you nor your heirs will be held financially responsible if your loan balance exceeds your home's value.

As with all reverse mortgages, Federal law requires lenders to give borrowers a three-day "right-of-rescission". Even after you sign the final paperwork at closing, you still have three days (including Saturdays, but not Sundays) to change your mind without any type of penalty. However, your funds will not available until the end of the three-day period, nor will interest be charged on your loan balance.

Eligibility

The HECM product includes eligibility requirements beyond the general requirements covered in chapter 1, including the no-cost counseling requirement.

CAIVRS

The Credit Alert Interactive Voice Response System (CAIVRS) is a Federal database of delinquent debtors. If you are delinquent on a debt related to a federal agency (such as a VA-guaranteed mortgage, Federal student loan, Small Business Administration loan, or Title I loan), your social security number is added to this database.

Your lender will check this list for your social security number. If your number appears, you will not be able to receive a HECM (or Home Keeper) reverse mortgage or any type of federal loan. Your social security number must be removed from CAIVRS for at least 36 months before you are eligible for any HUD-insured loan or mortgage.

LDP and GSA

If you have ever been suspended, debarred, or excluded from any HUD programs, you are not eligible for a HECM. Your lender will check HUD's Limited Denial of Participation (LDP) List and the government's General Services Administration (GSA) list of parties Excluded from Federal Procurement or Nonprocurement Programs.

Minimum Property Standards

Under the HECM program, potential properties must meet HUD's minimum property standards (MPS). These standards were established as a guide for all buildings and homes that participate in HUD housing programs.

Because the collateral for the reverse mortgage is your home and nothing else, the FHA must take precautions to protect its "investment". Once you have completed the initial paperwork, an FHA-approved appraiser will inspect your home from the exterior paint to the kitchen cabinets and carpeting. If the appraiser discovers any deterioration in the interior and exterior of your home, it will be noted within the appraisal.

If the appraiser notes any physical conditions that do not meet HUD standards, you will be required to fix the problems before your reverse mortgage process is completed. Repairs estimated to be less than 15 percent of the maximum claim amount may be completed after closing. Required repairs over 15 percent of the maximum claim amount must be completed, inspected and approved prior to closing. If your required repairs total over 30 percent of the maximum claim amount, HUD will determine if your home is acceptable for a reverse mortgage.

For substantial required repairs, you may escrow the necessary funds and complete the repairs after closing. An estimate from a licensed contractor is generally required so the underwriter can set aside the amount needed in escrow. (Your lender may also set aside extra funds for inspections once the repairs have been completed. Lenders may also charge a repair administration fee to monitor post-closing repairs.)

Generally, the amount your lender sets aside for repairs will be higher than the amount of the contractor's estimate (usually 1.5 times). For Texas residents, state law specifies certain requirements for administration of escrowed money. Be sure to check with your lender.

If you escrow the money for required repairs, make sure the repairs are completed within the time specified in your loan agreement. If you fail to do so, you could be in violation of your loan agreements, and your lender may discontinue payments and/or freeze your line of credit.

Borrowing Limits

HUD has developed a special equation to determine the amount for which each homeowner is eligible. This is called your principal limit. Under the HECM program, HUD takes into account:

1. The youngest borrower's age,

2. The home's appraised value or the maximum claim amount for your geographic area (the lesser of the two), and

3. The expected mortgage interest rate.

Why does age matter? Because the longer you live, the longer you will receive monthly income and the longer you will pay servicing fees, interest, and mortgage insurance premiums. Age plays a major factor in the amount of money a homeowner is eligible to receive, and HUD assumes life expectancy to be 100 years.

FHA determines your area's maximum claim amount (which is also the maximum amount that HUD will pay on an insurance claim for your area). This is the maximum amount of equity FHA will allow you to take from your home. Your principal limit is equal to the lesser of your home's appraised value (calculated by an FHA-approved appraiser) or the maximum claim amount for single-family residences in your geographic area.

As of January 1, 2004, the maximum claim amounts range from $161,076 to $290,319 across the nation. The amount is primarily determined by rural or urban locations, as well as the area's cost of living.

For example, the 2004 maximum claim amount for Lake County, Florida, is $161,097. If a Lake County resident's home is appraised at $180,000, the area's maximum claim amount of $161,097 will be used to determine the principal limit for the homeowner.

You should check your area's maximum loan amount before making any commitments on the HECM product. If your home's value is considerable higher than the maximum claim amount, a different reverse mortgage product may be a better option.

Information on how the interest rates are determined will be covered later in this chapter.

Balance Determination

Your reverse mortgage balance is equal to the total amount borrowed, plus interest and other costs (such as servicing fees, origination fees, insurance premiums, and, if applicable, costs from closing.)

Disbursement of Funds

With HECM products, you may obtain your reverse mortgage funds in the following manner:
1. Lump sum,
2. Tenure plan,
3. Term plan,
4. Line of credit (except in Texas),
5. Modified term plan, or
6. Modified tenure plan.

With the lump sum option, you may take all or a portion of your available reverse mortgage funds. If any funds remain, you may receive the rest of your funds through the other available plans.

The tenure plan provides equal monthly payments for as long as you occupy the home as your primary residence.

With the term payment, you will select a specific amount of time during which you will receive equal monthly payments.

A line of credit allows you to receive unscheduled payments at your discretion. You chose the time and amount that money is withdrawn until the line of credit is exhausted.

You are not charged interest on the unused funds remaining in your line of credit. Interest is only calculated on the amount you withdraw (plus fees and interest). However, HECM products have a special creditline growth feature. This means that the unused funds are growing at a specified growth rate, allowing you more access to your home's equity.

For example, based on rates from January 17, 2004, the growth rate for the monthly adjustable product was 3.29 percent. The growth rate for the annually adjustable product was 3.89 percent.

The modified tenure plan combines a line of credit with equal monthly payments for as long as you occupy your home as primary residence. While the monthly amount you receive will be lower than with the "regular" tenure plan, you will have an available line of credit until the funds are exhausted.

The modified term plan combines a line of credit with monthly payments for a specified amount of time. Again, the monthly payments will be lowered, but you will have an available line of credit until the funds are exhausted.

At any time through the course of your reverse mortgage, you are allowed to change the disbursement plan, receive an unscheduled payment, suspend payments, establish or terminate a line of credit, or receive your remaining net principal limit.

Interest Rates

At time of publication, HECM products calculate interest by using the 1-Year U.S. Treasury Constant Maturity Rate. This rate changes weekly and is printed in the financial section of many newspapers.

You have two options with the HECM product: an annually adjusted interest rate or a monthly-adjusted interest rate. You must choose how your rate will be determined at closing. Once you have made your decision on how interest will be charged, it is permanent and unchangeable!

All interest rates are adjustable, so the rate itself will change. At time of publication, the HECM monthly product adjusts interest monthly based on the 1-year Treasury bill + a margin of 1.50. For example, if the T-bill rate is 1.36 percent, your interest rate is 2.86 percent (1.36 + 1.5).

Since the interest rate is adjustable, it will change each month. However, the HECM-monthly product has a lifetime cap of 10 percent above the initial rate. For example, if your interest rate was 2.86 percent at closing, you can never be charged a higher rate than 12.86 percent.

The HECM annual program currently calculates the interest on a yearly basis, based on the 1-year Treasury bill + a margin of 2.10, with a 2 percent annual cap and a 5 percent lifetime cap. Using 1.36 as the sample T-bill rate, your interest would be 3.46 percent (1.36 + 2.10). Next year, the maximum value of your interest rate would be 5.46 percent (3.46 + 2), and, throughout the life of your reverse mortgage, the lifetime interest rate would be no higher than 8.46 percent (3.46 + 5).

HECM Interest Rates

- Two Options: Adjusted annually or monthly
- Based on 1-year Treasury bill plus a margin
- Lifetime caps on rates

Related Costs

With HECM reverse mortgages, you are always charged the same basic fees:

1. An origination fee,
2. Mortgage insurance premiums,

3.   Various closing costs,

4.   Servicing fees, and

5.   Interest.

Depending on your location, other fees may include, but are not limited to:

1.   An appraisal fee,

2.   Credit report fee,

3.   Courier fee,

4.   Title examination fee,

5.   Trust Review fee,

6.   County recording fees,

7.   City/County tax stamps,

8.   Property survey,

9.   Termite clearance letter,

10. Repair administration fee, and

11. Septic/Well/Gas line inspection.

(For an explanation of these costs, see Chapter 5 – Costs.)

The HECM allows you to finance most of your costs, which means the charges may be paid from the proceeds of your reverse mortgage. While financing costs lowers your out-of-pocket expenses, they also reduce the amount of reverse mortgage funds available to you.

Your lender may require you to pay for certain third-party items in advance such as:

-   Property appraisals,

-   Inspections,

-   Credit reports, and

-   Services performed by third parties.

Though you may be required to pay these in advance, it is possible to have these costs reimbursed at closing and added to your loan balance. However, you will pay interest on any cost calculated into your balance.

CHAPTER 2 SUMMARY

Product Profile

- The choice of over 95% of borrowers
- FHA insured

Disbursement of Funds

- Tenure Plan
- Term Plan
- Line of Credit
- Modified Tenure
- Modified Term

Quick Comparison Chart

	HECM	**HomeKeeper**
Payment Plans (Varies in Texas)	- Lump Sum - Tenure - Term - Line of Credit - Modified Tenure - Modified Term	- Lump Sum - Tenure - Line of Credit - Modified Tenure
Loan Limits	Varies by Location*	$ 333,700**
Calculating Age	- Age of Youngest Borrower - Average Expected Interest Rate - Maximum Claim Amount	- Number of Borrowers - Age of Borrowers - Adjusted Property Value

Line of credit option is not available to residents of Texas.

For 2004, loan limits range from $161,076 - $290,319. Contact a local lender to find out HUD's maximum claim amount for your area. Or, visit HUD's website at www.hud.gov.

** Fannie Mae's conventional loan limit at time of publication.

Fannie Mae is the largest non-bank financial services company in the world and listed as a New York Stock Exchange company.

In 1968, Fannie Mae became a private company operating with private capital on a self-sustaining basis. Its role was to purchase mortgages beyond traditional government loan limits, reaching a broader segment of Americans. Fannie Mae currently operates under a congressional charter, yet receives no government funding or backing.

Fannie Mae's mission, and ultimate goal, is to provide opportunities for more families to achieve homeownership. Since 1968, the company has provided $5.7 trillon in mortgage financing for 58 million families, making it the nation's largest source of financing home mortgages.

Product Profile

Fannie Mae's proprietary reverse mortgage product, called the Home Keeper Mortgage, has been available to seniors since 1995. While the Home Keeper has many similarities to the HECM (reviewed in chapter 2), both products have different features and benefits that anyone considering a reverse mortgage should understand. In some cases, average or above-average valued homes may be eligible for a higher cash advance or monthly payment through Fannie Mae.

Fannie Mae backs the Home Keeper Mortgage, just like FHA insures the HECM option. In other words, if your lender fails to make the agreed upon payment, Fannie Mae ensures that you receive your reverse mortgage funds.

As with all reverse mortgages, if you chose the Home Keeper Mortgage option, Federal law allows you a three-day right of rescission. This means you have three days (including Saturdays, but not Sundays) from the time you sign the closing paperwork to change your mind, regardless of the reason. Your funds will not be available until after this three-day period, so plan accordingly.

Eligibility

The Home Keeper Mortgage follows the same general reverse mortgage requirements explained in Chapter 1. In addition to these requirements, your property must meet Fannie Mae's standard housing requirements (which covers single-family houses, condominiums, and townhouses). Mortgage loans secured by manufactured housing, cooperative housing, and two to four-unit properties are ineligible.

You must receive reverse mortgage counseling by a nonprofit or public agency counselor approved by Fannie Mae. Your counseling may take place in person or, if you are unable or unwilling to travel, over the telephone. The counselor will:

- Explain the Home Keeper Mortgage,
- Review your responsibilities,
- Review estimated loan advances and costs, and
- Compare the benefits of the Home Keeper to other reverse mortgage options.

You, and all co-borrowers, must be at least 62 years of age and occupy the home as your primary residence. Up to three co-borrowers are allowed per reverse mortgage.

You must own your home or have a relatively low mortgage balance on your property. As with the HECM option, any existing mortgage debt must be retired before your reverse mortgage is complete. However, you may take a cash advance at your reverse mortgage closing to satisfy your current mortgage.

An approved appraiser will thoroughly examine your home, note any repairs that are needed, and estimate the value of your home. Similar to HECM, if your home requires repairs, you may be required to fix the problems before your reverse mortgage closing.

Borrowing Limits

With the HECM option, the borrowing limits vary by location, with the highest maximum claim amount in the country at $290,319 (at time of publication). If your home value falls above the HECM limit, you may be eligible for a larger amount of funds through Fannie Mae.

Fannie Mae determines the available amount, or your principal limit, by calculating three variables:
- The age & number of borrowers,
- The value of your property, and
- The adjusted property value,

When determining your principal limit, your age and life expectancy account for a large factor in fund eligibility. Loan payments to a single borrower will be more than to a couple with identical ages. According to Fannie Mae, couples statistically have a longer combined life expectancy than single borrowers. Longer life expectancy means lower monthly payments for a longer amount of time. If there are three co-borrowers, the two youngest borrowers' ages are used.

After you complete the reverse mortgage counseling session, an approved appraiser will evaluate your home to determine the value of your property.

The "adjusted property value" is similar to FHA's maximum claim amount. This is the maximum amount of funds Fannie Mae will lend, or your principal limit. Fannie Mae bases its maximum loan amounts on the average home price throughout the United States. So, through a Home Keeper Mortgage, the available funds will be the lesser of your property value or Fannie Mae's maximum loan amount. (At time of publication, Fannie Mae's conventional loan limit was $333,700.)

Home Keeper
Fast Fact

For higher valued homes, Fannie Mae's Home Keeper may offer more available funds.

For example, if your home is valued at $375,000, then the adjusted property value is $333,700. Even though your home is worth more than the maximum amount, your reverse mortgage funds will be based on Fannie Mae's limit of $333,700.

Balance Determination

Your Home Keeper Mortgage balance is equal to the total amount you receive, including the amount borrowed, interest and other costs (such as servicing fees, origination fees, and other costs that were not paid in cash at closing).

With a reverse mortgage, your balance will grow on a monthly basis because of interest and servicing fees. But, remember you can never owe more than the value of your home.

Disbursement of Funds

At your reverse mortgage closing, you will have three options regarding the way you receive your funds:

- Tenure plan,
- Line of credit plan, or
- Modified tenure plan.

The tenure payment plan provides you with equal monthly payments while the home remains your primary residence.

The line of credit plan allows you to receive funds at any time, in any amount, until your funds have been exhausted. If you desire a cash lump sum, you may chose the line of credit option and withdraw all the funds.

Fannie Mae's line of credit option differs from the HECM line of credit. Unlike the HECM, the Home Keeper Mortgage's line of credit does not offer a growth rate for the unused funds.

The modified tenure plan allows you to receive equal monthly payments and develop a line of credit. If you choose this option, your monthly payment will be lowered to allocate funds into your line of credit.

(In Texas, there are specific state laws regarding the disbursement of funds, and the line of credit option is not available.)

Once you have selected your disbursement option, it is possible to change that plan. Be aware that you may be charged a fee of no more than $50 to make such a change.

If you receive monthly payments, the Home Keeper Mortgage

also allows you to suspend those payments for a designated period. Even though you may put your payments on hold, the monthly fees and interest on your reverse mortgage balance will continue to be added to your loan balance during the suspended time.

Interest Rates

As with other reverse mortgage products, the Home Keeper Mortgage carries an adjustable interest rate. This means that the interest rates may be adjusted within a particular range and time.

At time of publication, the Home Keeper Mortgage calculated interest based on the 1-month secondary market CD index plus a margin. Since the rate of the CD rate changes monthly, your interest rate will change monthly. However, there is a lifetime cap of 12 percent over the life of the loan. So, if your reverse mortgage's interest rate is 6 percent, it can never exceed 18 percent.

Related Costs

Home Keeper Mortgages always have the same basic charges:
- An origination fee,
- Various closing costs, and
- A monthly servicing fee.

The origination fee is the same as the HECM product. A lender cannot charge more than $2,000 or 2 percent of the adjusted property value, whichever is greater. This fee may be financed into your reverse mortgage.

Closing costs vary from one location to another but generally cover services that are necessary to complete the reverse mortgage process.

Closing costs may include, but are not limited to:

- Appraisal,
- Title search & title insurance,
- Credit report,
- Termite inspection,
- Flood zone certificate,
- Document preparation,
- State & county recording fees,
- Attorney's fees,
- Intangible tax, and
- State residential funding fees.

The Home Keeper Mortgage allows you to finance all closing costs into your reverse mortgage balance. However, many lenders require a cash payment for items performed by third parties – such as appraisals and inspections.

The servicing fee covers costs associated with the administration of your reverse mortgage on a month-to-month basis. Your lender determines this flat fee, but Fannie Mae has capped the fee at $35 per month. You can expect a servicing fee around $30 to $35 per month.

Repayment

Your loan becomes due and payable when one of the following occurs:

- Upon your death, or the death of the last surviving borrower;
- If you sell the home;
- If you, or last surviving borrower, have not occupied the home as your primary residence for the majority of the year;
- If you are unable or refuse to repair the property; or

- If you fail to meet the obligations outlined in your loan agreement (such as property taxes, homeowners insurance, etc.)

In some cases, a lender will assist in some way if you are unable to pay property taxes or repair your property. Your lender is interested in collecting on its investment, not collecting your home. However, if you do not work together to find a solution, you could possibly lose your home (similar to traditional mortgages).

For additional termination and repayment guidelines, review chapter one.

If you chose the Home Keeper Mortgage, you may prepay all or part of the loan balance without a prepayment penalty. In some cases, this may work to your advantage because it reduces the outstanding balance. Regardless of the reason for prepayment, you will increase the net principal limit that is available to you.

CHAPTER 3 SUMMARY

Product Profile

- Preferred option for homes valued over FHA's maximum claim amount
- Interest based on 1-month secondary market CD rate

Disbursement of Funds

- Tenure Plan
- Line of credit
- Modified tenure

Product Profile

The home purchase option is a special feature, offered only by Fannie Mae, to help seniors purchase a home with reverse mortgage funds. Whether you are downsizing or purchasing a handicap accessible home, with the *Home Keeper for home purchase*, you may purchase a home without depleting your personal resources.

The Home Keeper for home purchase is ideal for seniors who:

1. Do not want a monthly mortgage payment on a home, and/or
2. Do not want to use a large amount of personal funds to purchase a home.

The Home Keeper for home purchase requires seniors to make a small down payment. If possible, it uses reverse mortgage funds to cover the remaining balance of the purchase price. (The amount of down payment necessary varies by age. The older your age the less funds you are required to use as a down payment.)

Because this is a purchase transaction, the 3-day right of rescission period is *not* applicable.

The home purchase option is a variation of Fannie Mae's Home Keeper Mortgage and only used for purchasing a home. The interest

REAL LIFE EXAMPLE 4-1

Mrs. Jones
Single Home Buyer
Age **76**

Purchase Price of
Desired Home:
$ 180,000

With Fannie Mae's home purchase option,
Mrs. Jones qualifies to borrow $123,000.

SCENARIO:

Mrs. Jones wishes to purchase her new
home and have no mortgage payments.

Option A:

Mrs. Jones takes $180,000 from the sale of her old house and
her savings account and purchases the home with cash; thus,
no mortgage payments.

Option B:

Mrs. Jones obtains a Home Keeper mortgage for $123,000
and combines with $57,000 from savings; thus, no mortgage
payments. The reverse mortgage is not due until she no longer
occupies the home as primary residence.

Mrs. Jones retains an extra $123,000.

- -

*The above numbers are calculated based upon rates from
May 2003. Changes in applicant's age, home value, and
interest rates may cause available amounts to be higher or
lower than stated.*

rate determination, cost and repayment are similar to the Home Keeper Mortgage.

Eligibility

With a Home Keeper Mortgage for home purchase, you must have a relatively low mortgage balance on your current home. And, similar to a traditional mortgage, you must provide fund verification on all monies used in your down payment.

Because reverse mortgages must be the first lien on a property, you will not be able to apply for a reverse mortgage and a traditional mortgage together. In other words, if you cannot purchase the new property by combining your down payment, reverse mortgage funds, and/or funds from your previous home's sale, you are not eligible for the home purchase feature.

The potential property must meet Fannie Mae's standard guideline requirements. Mortgages secured by manufactured housing, cooperative housing, and multiple-unit properties are not eligible.

You must complete the free counseling session with an approved counselor or counseling agency. The counselor will review with you the obligations of your reverse mortgage. Once you have completed the in-person or telephone counseling requirement, you must return your original counseling certificate to your lender. Only then may processing begin.

Borrowing Limits

Once you have decided on the home purchase feature, you must identify your desired home and ask your lender to estimate the reverse mortgage amount. Fannie Mae uses a formula to calculate the reverse mortgage amount for which you are eligible by taking into account:

- Age,
- Number of borrowers, and
- Adjusted property value (the lesser of the appraised value or Fannie Mae's current loan limit).

The sales price listed in the sales contract is used to estimate the available amount of reverse mortgage funds. However, at closing, the appraised value will be used as the actual property value for the final calculation of funds.

For example, if you purchase a home for $150,000, but the appraiser values your home at $152,500, your reverse mortgage funds will be calculated using the $152,500 value.

Disbursement of Funds

If you utilize the home purchase option, your reverse mortgage funds will be available only as a line of credit. You access a lump sum draw from your line of credit at your closing. This is to be used as purchase funds. If any funds remain, you may keep them in the line of credit.

Steps for utilizing the home purchase feature:

1. Identify new property & negotiate home purchase price.
2. Complete the Home Keeper Mortgage application and origination process.
3. Identify all funds used for financing following standard verification procedures. (Gift funds are acceptable.)

4. Home Keeper Mortgage documents are signed at closing, and you receive the deed to your new home. You are required to occupy your new primary residence within 30 days of closing.

CHAPTER 4 SUMMARY

Product Profile
- Used to purchase a home only
- Three-day right of rescission not applicable
- Down payment funds are required

Disbursement Plan
- Line of Credit

Financial Freedom Senior Funding Corporation, a subsidiary of Lehman Brothers Bank, FSB, is currently the largest reverse mortgage lender and servicer in the United States.

The Cash Account™ Plan is Financial Freedom's proprietary reverse mortgage product, with Lehman Brothers Bank as the investor.

This type of reverse mortgage is primarily designed for homes with values over $500,000. The Cash Account™ plan is not available in all 50 states. Your local reverse mortgage lender can supply you with the options for your area.

Product Profile

While Fannie Mae and HUD have lower maximum borrowing limits, the Cash Account™ has no maximum home value limit. So, this is a popular option for those with homes valued high above HUD's and Fannie Mae's maximum lending limit.

The Cash account offers two options for reverse mortgage borrowers:

- Standard Option and
- Zero Point™ Option

Both options create a line of credit for the borrower, with unused funds growing annually. Funds are available after the three-day right

Standard Option

- Origination fee equals 2 percent of home's value
- Open-ended revolving line of credit
- Annual growth rate on unused funds
- $500 minimum draw

Zero Point™ *Option*

- No origination fee
- Must initually withdraw 75 percent of maximum available funds
- $500 minimum draw
- Capped closing costs
- Partial prepayment not allowed during first 5 years
- Annual growth rate on unused funds

of rescission. Any existing mortgage balance must be paid off with your reverse mortgage funds prior to the release of money.

Eligibility

To qualify for the Cash Account™ product, you must meet the general eligibility requirements outlined in Chapter 1. In addition to those requirements, the minimum value of your home must be $75,000.

Eligible home types include:

- Single-family detached homes,
- Condominiums,

- Manufactured homes, and
- One-to-four unit rentals (if owner occupies one unit).

Ineligible home types include:

- Mobile homes,
- Co-ops
  (except in New York City),
- Second homes,
- Commercial properties, and
- Agriculture properties.

For the Zero Point™ Option only, borrowers are required to withdraw 75 percent of the maximum amount available at closing. However, there is no origination fee and closing costs have a maximum cap. There is no prepayment penalty for repaying any of the funds early; however, you may not make any repayments until the mortgage has been in effect for five years.

As with all reverse mortgage products, you must attend counseling by an independent, approved counselor. Your obligations related to obtaining a Cash Account™ will be reviewed in this one-time, no-cost session.

Borrowing Limits

The Cash Account™ allows you to borrow a higher maximum amount than any other reverse mortgage product. While no maximum lending limit is set, each individual property is considered on a case-by-case basis to determine the limit.

Disbursement Options

The Cash Account offers you two payment options- an open-ended revolving line of credit or scheduled payments. When withdrawing funds from the line of credit, you must remove a minimum of $500 per draw.

The Zero Point Option requires you to immediately withdraw 75 percent of the funds available to you; the Standard Option does not.

Interest Rates

Both Cash Account™ options use the same calculation for interest – LIBOR plus a margin. LIBOR is the London InterBank Offered Rate and is used as a base index for determining adjustable rate mortgages. The LIBOR is determined from information available at 11:00 am (London) on the second to last business day of every month. The rate is based on U.S. dollar deposits of a stated maturity calculated by a specified group of London banks.

The interest rate is reset twice a year and has a lifetime cap (6 percent at time of publication).

Related Costs

The Cash Account allows you to finance your closing costs into your reverse mortgage balance. Your costs may include, but are not limited to:

- An appraisal fee,
- Credit report,
- Tax service contract fee,

- Flood certification,
- Title search,
- Processing fee,
- Title insurance,
- State & county recording fees,
- Intangible tax,
- Survey (if required), and
- Termite/pest inspection.

Depending on the option you chose, some charges may vary.

Standard Option

- Origination fee of 2 percent of home's value

Zero Point Option

- No Origination Fee
- Capped closing costs (not including local or state taxes, if applicable)

Repayment

There is no prepayment penalty with either Cash Account option. However, with the Zero Point Option, you cannot repay any funds for at least five years.

CHAPTER 5 SUMMARY

Product Profile
- No maximum home value limit
- Minimum home value of $75,000
- Zero Point ™ option has no origination fee
- Interest calculated by LIBOR plus margin

Disbursement Plans
- Line of credit only
- Zero Point ™ option requires initial draw of 75 percent of available funds

A s with many financial products, circumstances may occur that require special attention. It would be virtually impossible to cover all of these situations, so we will focus on the most common.

Required Repairs

While performing the appraisal, an appraiser may find damage that prevents your home from meeting HUD's or Fannie Mae's minimum acceptable level of quality. (About half of the homes in the reverse mortgage program have required some form of home repair due to the average age of the applicants' homes.) If this occurs, you will be required to repair the damage and, in some cases, before your reverse mortgage may close. You may be required to obtain estimates of the repair cost from contractors in your area.

Required repairs that are more than 15 percent of the maximum claim amount must be completed, inspected and approved prior to closing. Some contractors will wait to receive payment for their services from your reverse mortgage funds at closing. However, many contractors may request the funds once the work is completed.

Required repairs that are less than 15 percent of your maximum claim amount may be completed after closing. You will sign a Repair Rider to the Loan Agreement, which outlines your responsibilities for completing the repairs in a satisfactory manner. If you do not follow these guidelines, you could put yourself in violation of your reverse mortgage terms, and the mortgage could become due and payable.

Your lender will set aside at least 150 percent of the total cost of repairs. These funds will not be available to you until the repairs have been completed. Your lender is allowed to charge you an administrative fee, which is separate from any fees that you pay for compliance inspections.

For required repairs over 30 percent of the maximum claim amount, you and/or your lender will need to work with a HUD representative to determine if your property qualifies for a reverse mortgage.

Living Trust

Revocable living trusts (or inter vivos trusts) on properties are eligible, as long as they meet certain requirements.

A living trust is created when the homeowner imparts the property to a trust, but continues to hold the equitable title. The trust holds legal title to the property. The homeowner may name himself/herself as the beneficiary.

Properties held in a living trust are eligible for a reverse mortgage if the following conditions are meet:

- All beneficiaries must be eligible reverse mortgage borrowers (Contingent beneficiaries do not need to be eligible.);
- The trust cannot be a party to the loan agreement; and
- The trust must be valid and enforceable, and it must

provide the lender assurance that it will be notified of any occupancy changes.

Issues with trusts tend to be complicated. It is wise to speak with a financial and/or legal advisor about the effects of reverse mortgages on trusts.

Life Estate

A life estate allows the homeowner to reside in the property for his or her lifetime. Once deceased, the homeowner leaves a fee simple title to the property to the individual(s) - including commercial or nonprofit organizations - named in the estate.

Properties in life estates are eligible under certain conditions. Check with your lender to determine eligibility.

Manufactured Homes

A manufactured home is defined as:
- A structure that can be transported in one or more sections;
- The structural part of the home is a trailer; and
- The weight of the home is on one beam.

Manufactured homes are eligible for reverse mortgages if they comply with the following conditions:
1. The home must have been constructed after June 15, 1976;
2. The floor area of the home must be at least 400 square feet;
3. The home must conform to the Manufactured Home

Construction & Safety Standards and bear the certification label (Only homes built after June 15, 1976 will have this label.);

4. The classification and taxation of the home must be listed as real estate;

5. The home may not have been occupied or installed in any other site;

6. The foundation must be inspected by a licensed engineer prior to the appraisal to confirm that it meets HUD guidelines;

7. The axles and tongues must be removed;

8. Permanent utilities must be installed;

9. A permanent skirt must surround the perimeter; and

10. The finished grade elevation beneath the home or the lowest finished exterior grade must be at or above the 100-year return frequency flood elevation.

If located in a cooperative housing development, the home is not eligible. The home is also ineligible if it qualifies for HUD's Special Risk Insurance Fund.

Modular Homes

Confusing a modular home with a manufactured home is easy. With a modular home, the trailer is not a structural part of the home, and external foundation walls support the weight.

Modular homes are not required to meet the manufactured home requirements listed above.

Condominiums

Condominiums must be listed on an approved condo list to be eligible for a reverse mortgage. If your building is not currently listed, it is possible to become eligible by having your homeowners' association complete a spot condo approval form, which is required by HUD and Fannie Mae. You may be required to produce a copy of the homeowners' association's current and previous year's budget.

The following are several general requirements:

1. If the building contains over 50% of rental units, the property is not eligible.
2. If a recreation lease is in place, the property is not eligible.
3. The homeowners' association must provide a copy of the blanket insurance policy declarations' page to prove it has the correct coverage amount for the minimum standards (full coverage of buildings and liability of $1,000,000).

Even if the condominium structure has previously been approved, confirmation that 51 percent of the units are owner-occupied is still necessary.

Private Roads & Shared Driveways

Vehicles and pedestrians must have access to your property by public or private road. If you must travel down a private road to gain access to your home, the road must meet the following requirements:

1. The surface must allow passable access to passenger and emergency vehicles at all times;

2. A permanent recorded easement or ingress/egress must be protected on the deed and on file with your county's clerk of court office; and

3. All parties who use the private round of driveway must sign a legally-binding joint maintenance agreement that states how road maintenance costs will be shared. The agreement must also state that the agreement is transferable to heirs and future owners of the property. (California and Oregon are the only two states that do not require joint maintenance agreements.)

If any of the above circumstances apply, a lender may be able to assist you.

Excess Land

If you own more than five acres of land and such plots are not typical for your area, the area may be considered excess land.

Excess land will not be included in the appraised property value or used in the valuation of the reverse mortgage, and it must have a lower value than that of your home.

The excess land does not have to be removed from the title, but it cannot be subdivided after the reverse mortgage is complete. If the land is subdivided, the reverse mortgage will require repayment.

Homestead Advisory

When a spouse or other party listed on the title is ineligible to receive a reverse mortgage, a homestead advisory must be signed.

By signing the form, the party is removed from the title and relinquishes all legal claim over the property.

This could involve serious repercussions and should be discussed with a legal advisor and/or counselor before proceeding.

If someone is to be removed from the title, the following must take place:

1. The individual being removed must attend counseling;

2. A quit claim removing the individual must be recorded at closing; and

3. If you reside in a homestead state, the individual being removed must still sign the new deed.

Homestead States

Even if your spouse will not be included in the reverse mortgage, if you reside in a homestead state, both husband and wife must sign the deed at closing. Homestead states include:

Alabama	Louisiana	Ohio
Arizona	Massachusetts	Oklahoma
Arkansas	Michigan	Pennsylvania
California	Minnesota	South Dakota
Colorado	Missouri	Tennessee
D.C.	Montana	Texas
Florida	New Hampshire	Vermont
Idaho	New Jersey	Washington
Illinois	New Mexico	West Virginia
Kansas	North Carolina	Wisconsin
Kentucky	North Dakota	Wyoming

Leaseholds

A leasehold occurs when the borrower has a lease agreement with a third party who owns the land. Not all leaseholds are eligible for reverse mortgages.

The property must be held in fee simple (meaning ownership subject only to governmental restrictions) or under a renewable lease for at least 99 years. A lease that has a term of at least 50 years beyond the 100th birthday of the youngest borrower is also eligible.

Your lender will need to review the lease to ensure that it meets all guidelines before determining your property's eligibility.

Power of Attorney, Conservator & Guardianship Issues

All issues related to power of attorney, conservator, and guardianship must follow the guidelines listed below.

If the borrower is legally competent:

- The borrower must sign the loan application; and
- A representative holding durable power of attorney designed to survive incapacity may execute the loan application.

If the borrower lacks legal competency:

- The borrower may not sign the loan application;
- The counseling session must be held with the individual holding power of attorney or the court-appointed conservator or guardian;
- With proper evidence of authority, a conservator or guardian may execute all necessary paperwork;
- A durable power of attorney authorized to survive

incapacity may execute all the necessary paperwork; and

- The durable power of attorney must follow state laws regarding signatures, notarization, witnesses, and recordation.

Wells & Septic Systems

If your property contains a well, the water must be tested for five elements – lead, nitrates, nitrites, total coliform and fecal coliform. The well must be located at least 15 feet from the house and at least 10 feet from your property lines. If a septic is located on the property, the distance between the well and septic tank must be at least 50 feet.

Septic inspections are required only if the appraiser notes a problem on the appraisal.

If you share a well or septic system with any neighboring properties, a recorded agreement between all involved parties must be signed and approved by your local authority. This agreement must also meet FHA guidelines. No more than 4 houses may share the same well.

If you have a community well, you must submit a copy of state or county permits and licenses.

If public utilities and sewer are available, you will be required to hook into the system, unless the cost (including the tap fee) exceeds 3 percent of your property's value.

Space Heaters & Wood Stoves

If your house is heated by a space heater, the appraiser must ensure that it is installed properly and meets all local fire codes. The appraiser must also note if the heater is typical for the area and adequate to service the entire house.

To ensure proper installation and determine if local fire codes are met, the appraiser must also inspect wood stoves.

Texas Residents

In the state of Texas, the reverse mortgage program has some differences in rules and regulations due to state laws. If you reside in Texas, check with a local lender to review state requirements. Some exceptions exist:

- Reverse mortgage funds may only be distributed on the first of every month; and
- If a power of attorney is used for closings, it must be the spouse.

Other differences relate to property charges (taxes and insurance), required repairs, and monthly servicing fees.

Financial Freedom's Cash Account™ is not available in Texas. Neither are the line of credit options with the HECM and Home Keeper Mortgage.

Funds may only be disbursed as follows:

- An initial lump sum advance,
- Monthly payments as long as one borrower occupies the home as the primary residence (tenure plan),
- Monthly payments for a specified amount of time

(term plan),

- A partial initial lump sum advance and tenure payments (modified tenure plan), and

- A partial initial lump sum advance and term payments (modified term payment plan).

Reverse mortgage funds are only disbursed on the first business day of each month for Texas residents.

If the borrower wishes to receive a lump sum payment, the funds must be withdrawn at the closing. Texas does not permit disbursement of any additional lump sum payments.

You may prepay your reverse mortgage funds at any time. (Full repayment equals termination of the mortgage.) For the HECM only, you may request a recalculation of monthly or term payments based on these pre-paid funds. This is considered a payment plan change, and the only type of payment plan change that is allowed for Texas residents.

Safeguards were put into place to offer seniors an extra safety measure against illegal or unethical practices by lenders.

Payment Guarantee

If your lender fails to make payments, you will still receive your reverse mortgage funds. Depending on the option you chose, the funds may come through the backing of the government or a private entity. The federal government insures the HECM; Fannie Mae guarantees the Home Keeper Mortgage; Financial Freedom guarantees the Cash Account.

Non-Recourse Loan

A reverse mortgage is a non-recourse debt; this means the collateral for the debt may only be based on the value of your home. Other personal assets and property may not be used as collateral if the amount due at the end of the loan exceeds the value of your home. Therefore, your debt is limited only to the maximum value of your home.

Three-Day Right of Rescission

You have the legal right to cancel your reverse mortgage up to three business days after your closing. The only exception to this rule occurs when you are using the funds to purchase a new home.

To terminate the process, you must provide a written statement (or complete a form from your lender) in the form of a letter, fax, or telegram. Your lender must receive this statement before midnight of the third business day. You are not allowed to cancel in person or by telephone.

Capped Interest Rates

Because the interest rate is adjustable, each reverse mortgage program has designated a cap on the maximum interest rate charged. For example, if your interest rate at closing is 5 percent, and the product has a 5 percent cap, your interest rate will never rise above 10 percent.

The interest rate cap varies by product. Check with an area lender for the current rate caps.

Counseling

Since reverse mortgages can be difficult to understand, all applicants are required by law to participate in counseling before the processing of the reverse mortgage may begin. This one-time session may take place at the counselor's office or, if you are unable or unwilling to travel, by telephone. (However, during the reverse mortgage process, regulations require your originator, lender or counselor to meet with you face-to-face.)

Some issues you will discuss include:

- The advantages and disadvantages of reverse mortgage products;
- The financial obligations associated with reverse mortgages;
- How a reverse mortgage will affect taxes, eligibility assistance under Federal and State programs, and the estate and/or heirs; and
- Other home equity conversion options available to you, and/or local or state programs that may offer you financial assistance.

An approved, independent counselor must conduct the reverse mortgage counseling to ensure you receive unbiased information. The counselor does not work for your lender and cannot be compensated by your lender for this service.

In most cases, your lender will have a list of counselors to which they send reverse mortgage applicants. If you wish to find your own counselor, make sure he or she is HUD-approved or Fannie Mae-approved before agreeing to the session. And, make sure there is no charge for the counseling.

Counselors will also ask if you have signed a contract or been charged a fee by an estate planning firm. In previous years, some organizations have taken advantage of senior homeowners and charged fees for information that should have been available without charge. It is illegal for companies to charge any kind of estate planning fee related to reverse mortgages.

If family members or financial advisors wish to participate in your reverse mortgage process, they may be included in your counseling session. However, only the borrower(s) is required to participate.

Once counseling is complete, the counselor will send you an official certificate of completion. You will need to send the original certificate to your lender.

Total Annual Loan Cost (TALC) Disclosures

The true total annual loan cost of a reverse mortgages depends on three main factors:

- The length of your reverse mortgage,
- The advances you select, and
- Your home's appreciation rate.

Your lender must provide you with the Total Annual Loan Cost of your reverse mortgage. This calculation takes all of the costs and fees associated with your reverse mortgage and turns it into one annual average rate (including principal, interest, closing costs, servicing fees, and mortgage insurance premiums). While many variables may change and affect the total cost (such as your home's appreciation rate or interest rates), this is currently the most accurate way to measure the true total annual loan cost of your reverse mortgage.

The longer your reverse mortgage is in effect, and the more your home appreciates, the lower your TALC rate will be.

Within three days of signing and returning your initial reverse mortgage application, your lender is legally required to provide you with a "Good Faith Estimate of Settlement Costs". The amounts listed on this sheet reflect the charges that you are likely to incur during your reverse mortgage. These numbers are only estimates provided by your lender. The actual cost of these items will be disclosed at your closing. (In most cases, your lender cannot provide you with an exact number until work has been completed.)

Many of the costs associated with reverse mortgages are similar to those you find with traditional mortgages, such as an origination fee, appraisal fee, and closing costs. These costs and charges will vary depending on your location.

Different states have varying rules and regulations regarding fees related to any kind of mortgage. If you are unsure of a particular fee, check with your lender, financial advisor, and/or reverse mortgage counselor.

Origination Fee

The origination fee is charged by your lender and covers the cost of "originating" or setting up your reverse mortgage. Legally, lenders may not charge more than two percent (2%) of your home's appraised value or two percent of your county's maximum claim amount, whichever is less. The minimum origination fee is $2,000. So, if two percent of your home's value is less than $2,000, your lender may raise the origination fee to $2,000. (Federal law governs origination fee amounts.)

Appraisal Fee

An appraisal of your home is required and used as the basis for calculating the amount of reverse mortgage funds available to you.

A licensed appraiser will examine your home and provide a professional opinion of its market value based upon location, condition, and surrounding home values.

The cost for an appraisal varies by location. Because this fee is paid to a third-party, your lender may require you to cover this cost in advance. If you have paid the fee, you have the right to receive a copy of your home's appraisal. Your lender can provide this to you.

Credit Report Fee

Credit is not a requirement for a reverse mortgage. Your lender will primarily use the credit report to determine if any liens are held against your property. This report allows your lender to quickly verify your current mortgage balance, if applicable. Lenders also check for bankruptcies, judgments against the property, and defaulted government loans.

If any liens against the property exist, you must satisfy the charges before you are eligible to receive any funds. In some cases, these liens may be paid at closing using reverse mortgage funds.

The credit report fee is another charge that may vary by lender. (Fannie Mae's Home Keeper Mortgage does not require a credit report.)

Hazard Insurance

Hazard (or homeowners) insurance is required on all reverse mortgages. The insured amount must equal the appraised value of your home less the site value or guaranteed replacement cost coverage. You are required to have the policy paid up for 90 days past your closing date.

Tax Service Fee

In some states, you are required to pay a tax on services (similar to sales tax on goods from a department store). So, you might have to pay a tax on the services performed by your lender, title company, and other third-party service providers.

This fee is only applicable in certain states. Check with your lender to see if you are affected by this tax.

FHA Mortgage Insurance Premium (HECM only)

As discussed in Chapter 2, the mortgage insurance premium offers financial protection for both you and your lender. Reverse mortgage participants are required to pay the insurance premiums in two ways – an upfront charge and an annual charge.

The upfront charge is the first insurance premium equal to two percent (2%) of your home's appraised value and may be financed into your reverse mortgage. The second premium, which is one-half percent (0.5%) of the mortgage balance per year, is added to your reverse mortgage balance on an annual basis.

Title Examination

To ensure your home's title is clear from any defects, the title company conducts a title examination. The cost of a title examination is based on the principal loan amount available to you and varies by location.

Title Insurance

Your deed is written evidence that you own your property. Title insurance protects you, as well as your lender, against financial losses due to any legal defects in the deed.

Title insurance includes:

- Assurance that no one else owns interest in your title,
- Protection against forgery & impersonation, and
- A guarantee that there is not an easement on the land or no one can claim a right to limit your use of land.

With the HECM, title insurance is based on the maximum claim amount times 150 percent. The Home Keeper Mortgage bases title insurance on the original principal limit times 150 percent.

Recording Fees

Recording fees cover the cost of filing your reverse mortgage document and mortgage note into official public record. These fees are paid to the clerk of court's office for the county in which the property is located. Check with your lender or county's clerk of courts office for current fee amounts.

Document Stamps

Required taxes, in the form of stamps, are charged when recording your mortgage with the county. The taxes vary by location; check with your lender or county's clerk of courts office for current fee amounts.

Property Survey

The survey is a legal description and drawing of your property. This verifies the precise physical location and property boundaries, including easements, encroachments, right of ways, and permanent fixtures (like your home, shed, or fence). The drawing is a sketch of the legal description.

The price of a survey varies by location. A survey is not required by all states.

Termite Clearance Letter

In almost every county nationwide, a clear termite letter is required (unless you reside in a condo above the first floor).

Termite clearance letters vary in price, depending upon your location. Clearance letters are valid for 90 days.

Repair Administration Fee

If you have required repairs that are completed after closing, you could be charged a repair administration fee of $50 or one and one half percent (1½%) of the repair estimate, whichever is greater.

Flood Insurance Certification

Flood certification is required if the property is located in a designated flood zone. Flood insurance is determined by subtracting your property's site value from your home's appraised value or the maximum flood insurance limit for your area.

Septic/Well/Gas Line Inspection

If the appraiser notes a problem with the septic, well, or gas line, an inspection may be required. The cost for these inspections varies by location.

Servicing Fee

The work your lender performs once the reverse mortgage has closed is called servicing. Servicing includes sending payments to you, making loan advances, transferring insurance premiums, sending regular account statements, verifying you have paid your taxes and insurance, etc.

FHA has limited the amount your lender may charge you to perform these services. At time of publication, if you chose the annually adjusted interest rate, your lender may not charge more than $30 per month.

With the monthly adjustable interest rate, your lender may not charge more than $35 per month.

Fannie Mae's and Financial Freedom's servicing fee may also vary and range from $25 to $35 per month.

Since reverse mortgages are calculated with a life expectancy of 100 years of age, FHA requires lenders to set aside, or withhold, the total amount of servicing fees you could potentially be charged. While lenders withhold this amount from your available balance, you are not charged the fee until the work has been performed for each month.

9 Application Process

In many cases, when contacting a lender to begin the reverse mortgage process, you will be sent a computer printout comparing the possible options available to you and the costs involved.

Pre-meeting preparation for your initial meeting with a lender may assist in speeding up the reverse mortgage process. Plan to provide your lender with the following items:

1. Picture identification (A clear, readable copy of a driver's license is sufficient.),

2. Evidence of date of birth (A clear, readable copy of driver's license is sufficient.),

3. Proof of social security number (Must be a clear, readable copy from your social security card, driver's license, birth certificate, or an official government-issue form.),

4. Property survey (This is not required by all states. An old survey of your property may save you from having to pay for another survey. Do not be concerned if you do not have one; your lender can easily order it.),

5. Evidence of hazard/homeowner insurance (include your policy number, agent's name and contact information), and

6. Copy of living trust (If your property is in a trust, it is wise to have your lender review it and determine eligibility early in the process.).

Your lender will provide you with a loan application and disclosure forms that you must sign. The disclosure forms include, but are not limited to:

- Good Faith Estimate of Settlement Costs,
- Required Providers List,
- Borrower's Notification,
- Servicing Transfer Disclosure,
- Tax & Insurance Disclosure,
- Loan Application,
- Repair Acknowledgement Form,
- Alternate Contact Form,
- Excessive Fees Disclosure, and
- Homestead Advisory (if applicable).

Once your loan application has been signed and submitted, your lender must provide you with a Good Faith Estimate of Settlement Costs within three days.

Your lender must obtain your original counseling certificate, which you receive once counseling is completed, before processing can begin. Processing includes the title search, appraisal, and credit check.

The lender will conduct a title search to ensure you are the property owner and that liens have not been filed against the property. As mentioned in a previous chapter, if liens are discovered, you must satisfy them at or before closing.

During the process, an appraiser will inspect your property to determine its market value. In some states, a survey is required to confirm your property's boundaries. The survey is also used to determine if your property is in a designated flood zone.

Once your lender has completed all the necessary processing, you will need to set up a time to close your loan, usually in the office of a local title company. Approximately one week before closing, your lender will contact you to confirm your choice of payment plan.

Because of the three-day right of rescission, you will not receive your reverse mortgage funds on the day of closing. During these three days, you may decide against a reverse mortgage for any reason. (You are not charged any interest on your reverse mortgage during these three days.) Saturdays are included in the three-day right of rescission, but not Sundays.

Your initial funds usually come in the form of a check in the mail. Remaining funds may come as a check, or, if you complete a form from your lender, direct deposit is available.

Glossary

Adjustable Interest Rate – the interest rate changes over time; based on a published market index

Adjusted Property Value – used to determine Fannie Mae's Home Keeper principal limit; equals the lower of the current loan limit or the home's appraised value

Appraisal – the estimated value of a property determined by a professional

Closing – typically held at a title company's office; borrower signs all legal documents to officially being the mortgage; also referred to as "settlement"

Closing Costs – cost to borrower for obtaining a reverse mortgage; includes origination fee, appraisal, title examination & insurance, etc. (See Chapter 8-Costs)

Counseling – a no-cost educational session performed by an independent source; topics covered include eligibility, costs, fund limits, responsibilities, and repayment

Credit Report – prepared by a credit bureau; an account of the applicant's credit history

Creditline – see Line of Credit

Deed – legal title to a property

Equity – the market value of the property minus current mortgage balance and/or debt against the home

Fannie Mae – a private, government-sponsored company that deals in mortgages; provides the Home Keeper Mortgage product

Federal Housing Administration (FHA) – a division of HUD; insurer of the HECM

Funding Date – the day the lender first provides funds; occurs after three day right-of-rescission

Hazard Insurance – provides protection against physical damage to property; generally covers hazards such as vandalism, high winds, fire, etc;

Home Equity – your property's value minus debt

Home Equity Conversion Mortgage (HECM) – HUD's reverse mortgage product

Home Equity Loan – allows homeowner to borrower funds based on home's equity; requires monthly repayments and credit & income requirements

Home Keeper Mortgage – Fannie Mae's reverse mortgage product

Homeowner's Insurance – merges hazard insurance with liability coverage

HUD – U.S. Department of Housing & Urban Development

Interest – the amount charges by lenders for borrowing funds

Loan Balance – the total amount due, including principal, interest, servicing fees, and financed closing costs

Lien – a debt with legal claim to property

Line of Credit – an account in which the borrower may withdraw reverse mortgage funds at any time; in many cases, the borrower may decide the minimum and maximum amount withdrawn

Loan Balance – the total outstanding amount due; equal to total amount borrowed plus financed closing costs, interest, servicing fees, insurance premiums, and other financed costs

Lump Sum – borrower receives a single cash payment, usually after three day right of rescission

Margin – a predetermined amount used to calculate interest rates

Maximum Claim Amount – the total amount that may be funded by FHA/HUD; equals the lower of the area's loan limit or the home's appraised value

Mortgage Insurance Premiums – fee for reverse mortgage insurance

Net Principal Limit - the amount of funds available over the course of the reverse mortgage

Non-Recourse Loan –lender is limited to the value of the property for repayment

Origination – the beginning step of the reverse mortgage process; documents preparation and file set up

Principal Limit – total amount of available funds at origination

Proprietary Reverse Mortgage – a private company's reverse mortgage product

Required Repairs – if noted in appraisal, these repairs that must be completed; untreated damage could devalue property

Reverse Mortgage – a special program for seniors over 62; provides borrowers with cash from home's equity

Right of Rescission – three days in which the borrower can cancel the loan without legal or financial consequences; three days includes Saturdays but not Sundays

Rising Debt – as funds are distributed and interest added, the total amount owed rises over time

Servicing – administrative work once your reverse mortgage is complete; includes sending checks and statements, paying taxes and insurance premiums, etc.

Survey – a legal description showing property's boundaries

Title – document that verifies legal ownership

Term Plan – provides equal monthly payments to borrower for a specific period of time

Tenure Plan – provides predetermined amount of funds every month until borrower no longer occupies home as primary residence

Total Annual Loan Cost (TALC) – the estimated annual cost of a reverse mortgage figured as a percentage; rate includes all costs

11 Appendix

Additional Resources

AARP

601 E Street NW

Washington, DC 20049

Telephone: (800) 424-3410

Hours: Monday - Friday, 8 am - 8 pm (EST)

Email: RMCounsel@aarp.org

Website: www.aarp.org/revmort

US Department of Housing & Urban Development (HUD)

451 7th Street SW

Washington, DC 20410

Telephone: (202) 708-1112

Website: www.hud.gov

Fannie Mae

3900 Wisconsin Avenue NW

Washington, DC 20016-2892

Telephone: (800) 7FANNIE

         (800-732-6643)

Hours: Monday - Friday, 9 am - 5 pm (EST)

Email: consumer_resources@fanniemae.com

Website: www.fanniemae.com

Additional Resources

Financial Freedom Senior Funding Corporation

7595 Irvine Center Drive

Suite 250

Irvine, CA 92618

Telephone: (888) REVERSE

        (888-738-3773)

Hours: Monday - Friday, 6 am - 5 pm (PST)

Email: sales@financialfreedom.com

Website: www.reversemortgage.com

National Reverse Mortgage Lenders Association (NRMLA)

1625 Massachusetts Avenue NW

Suite 601

Washington, DC 20036

Telephone: (202) 939-1760

Website: www.reversemortgage.org

National Center for Home Equity Conversion (NCHEC)

360 N Robert #403

Saint Paul, MN 55101

Website: www.reverse.org

Eligibility Checklist

Yes   No

Are you and all co-borrowers at
least 62 years old?
____   ____

Do you own your home?
____   ____

Is your home free and clear of
mortgage debt?
- or -
Do you have a relatively small
____   mortgage balance?   ____

Is the home your primary
residence?
____   ____

Will you attend a no-cost
____   counseling session?   ____

If you answered "Yes" to all of these questions, you have meet the general eligibility requirements for a reverse mortgage.

If you answered "No" to any of the above questions, you will need to speak with a qualified reverse mortgage lender to determine your eligibility.

Request Information

Borrower Information

Borrower: _____

Date of Birth: _____

Social Security Number: _____

Co-Borrower: _____

Date of Birth: _____

Social Security Number: _____

Property Information

Property Address: _____

_____

_____

County _____

Type of Property: ___ Single Family Residence ___ Condo ___ Manufactured Home ___ Townhouse ___ Other

Estimated Home Value: _____

Mortgage Balance: _____ 2nd _____

Year Built: _____ **How Long Owned?** _____

Send to: The Reverse Mortgage Handbook
Tara Ballman
P.O. Box 137621
Clermont, FL 34713

Or Email: Info@ReverseMortgageHandbook.com

Quick Order Form

Please send me ___ copies of *The Reverse Mortgage Handbook: A Consumer's Guide for Senior Homeowners* at $12.95 each.

Please send me more information on:
    ___ Other Books   ___ Info on Speaking/ Seminars

Name: _____

Address: _____

City: _____

State:_____ **Zip:** _____

    Payment: ___ **Check**   ___ **Credit Card**

    ____ Books at $12.95 each = _____
    Shipping Charges & Tax = _____
    Total Amount Due   = _____

Shipping: Add $4.00 for first book, $2.00 additional books.
Sales Tax: Florida residents only add 7%.

    Credit Card Orders: ___ **Visa**   ___ **MasterCard**

Card Number: _____

Name on Card: _____ **Exp.** _____

Signature: _____

— — — — — — — — — — — — — — — — — — —

Postal Orders: The Reverse Mortgage Handbook
                    P.O. Box 137621
                    Clermont, FL 34713
Fax Orders: (407) 396-4247
Email Orders: Orders@ReverseMortgageHandbook.com

Request Information

Borrower Information

Borrower: _____

Date of Birth: _____

Social Security Number: _____

Co-Borrower: _____

Date of Birth: _____

Social Security Number: _____

Property Information

Property Address: _____

_____

_____

County_____

Type of Property: ___ Single Family Residence ___ Condo
___ Manufactured Home ___ Townhouse ___ Other

Estimated Home Value:_____

Mortgage Balance: _____2nd _____

Year Built: _____ **How Long Owned?** _____

Send to: The Reverse Mortgage Handbook
Tara Ballman
P.O. Box 137621
Clermont, FL 34713

Or Email: Info@ReverseMortgageHandbook.com

Contact the Author

If you would like to contact the author to schedule speaking engagements, request additional information, or ask a reverse mortgage-related question, please send all correspondence to:

The Reverse Mortgage Handbook
Tara Ballman
P.O. Box 137621
Clermont, FL 34713
Email: Tara@ReverseMortgageHandbook.com

If you would like to contact the publisher for any reason, please send all correspondence to:

Jawbone Publishing Corporation
2907 Paddington Way
Kissimmee, FL 34747

Telephone: (407) 396-4245
Fax: (407) 396-4247

http://www.JawbonePublishing.com
Email: marketing@jawbonepublishing.com

Request Information

Borrower Information

Borrower: _____

Date of Birth: _____

Social Security Number: _____

Co-Borrower: _____

Date of Birth: _____

Social Security Number: _____

Property Information

Property Address: _____

_____

_____

County_____

Type of Property: ___ Single Family Residence ___ Condo
___ Manufactured Home ___ Townhouse ___ Other

Estimated Home Value:_____

Mortgage Balance: _____2nd _____

Year Built: _____ **How Long Owned?** _____

Send to: The Reverse Mortgage Handbook
                      Tara Ballman
                      P.O. Box 137621
                      Clermont, FL 34713

Or Email: Info@ReverseMortgageHandbook.com

Quick Order Form

Please send me ___ copies of *The Reverse Mortgage Handbook: A Consumer's Guide for Senior Homeowners* at $12.95 each.

Please send me more information on:
___ Other Books   ___ Info on Speaking/ Seminars

Name: _____

Address: _____

City: _____

State: _____ **Zip:** _____

Payment: ___ **Check**   ___ **Credit Card**

_____ Books at $12.95 each = _____

Shipping Charges & Tax = _____

Total Amount Due = _____

Shipping: Add $4.00 for first book, $2.00 additional books.
Sales Tax: Florida residents only add 7%.

Credit Card Orders: ___ **Visa**   ___ **MasterCard**

Card Number: _____

Name on Card: _____ **Exp.** _____

Signature: _____

— — — — — — — — — — — — — — — — — — — —

Postal Orders: The Reverse Mortgage Handbook
                 P.O. Box 137621
                 Clermont, FL 34713
Fax Orders: (407) 396-4247
Email Orders: Orders@ReverseMortgageHandbook.com